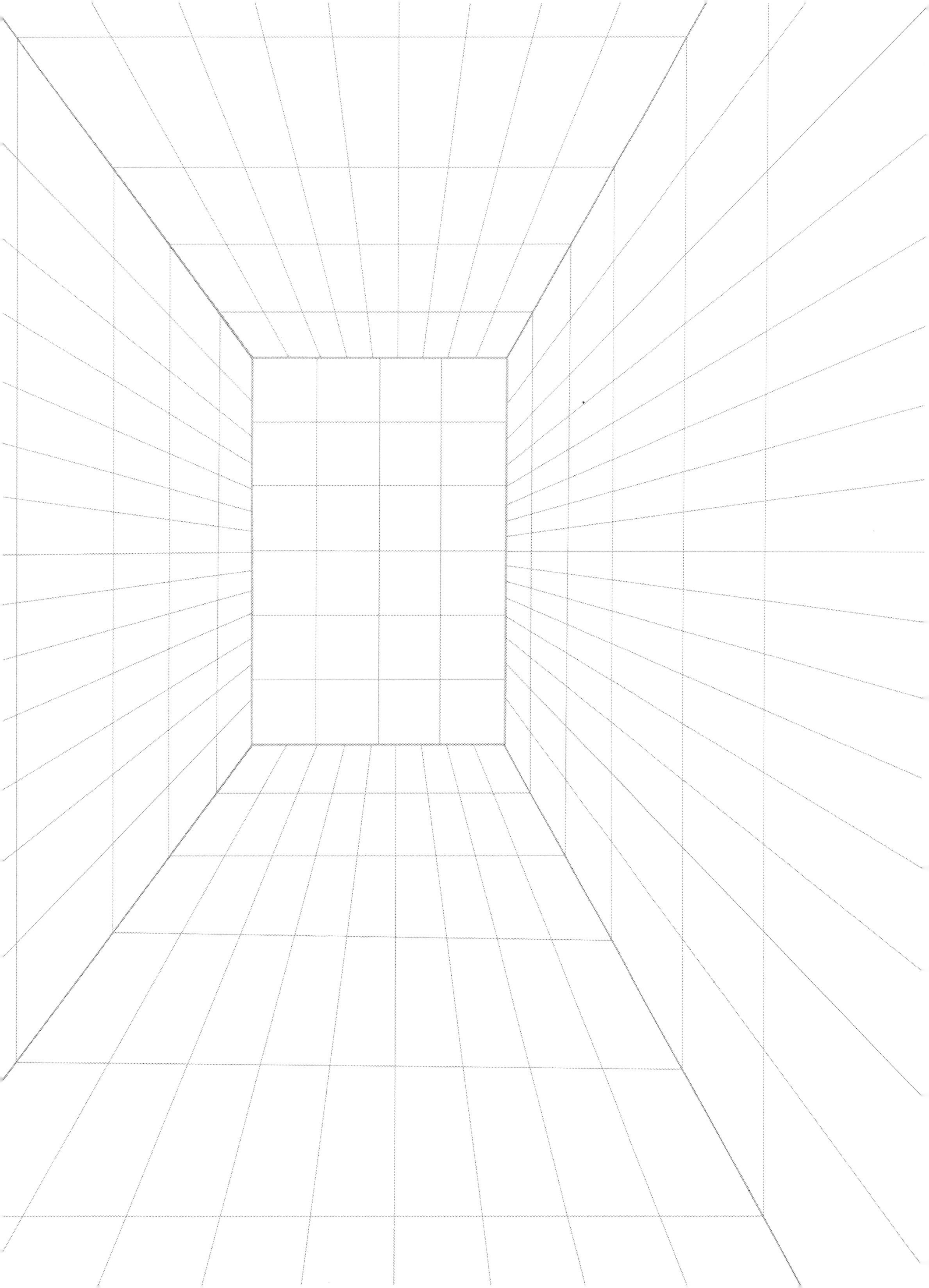

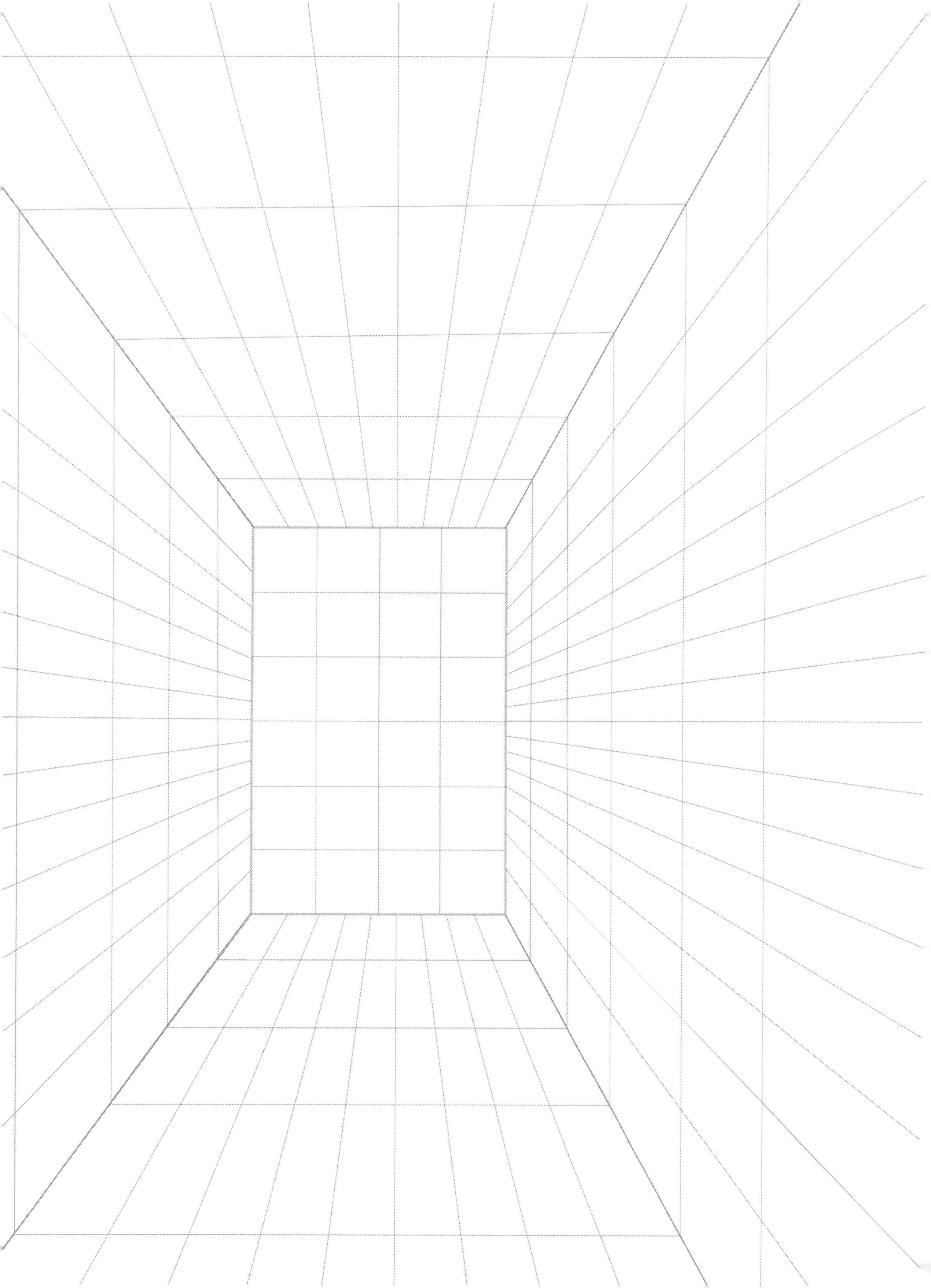

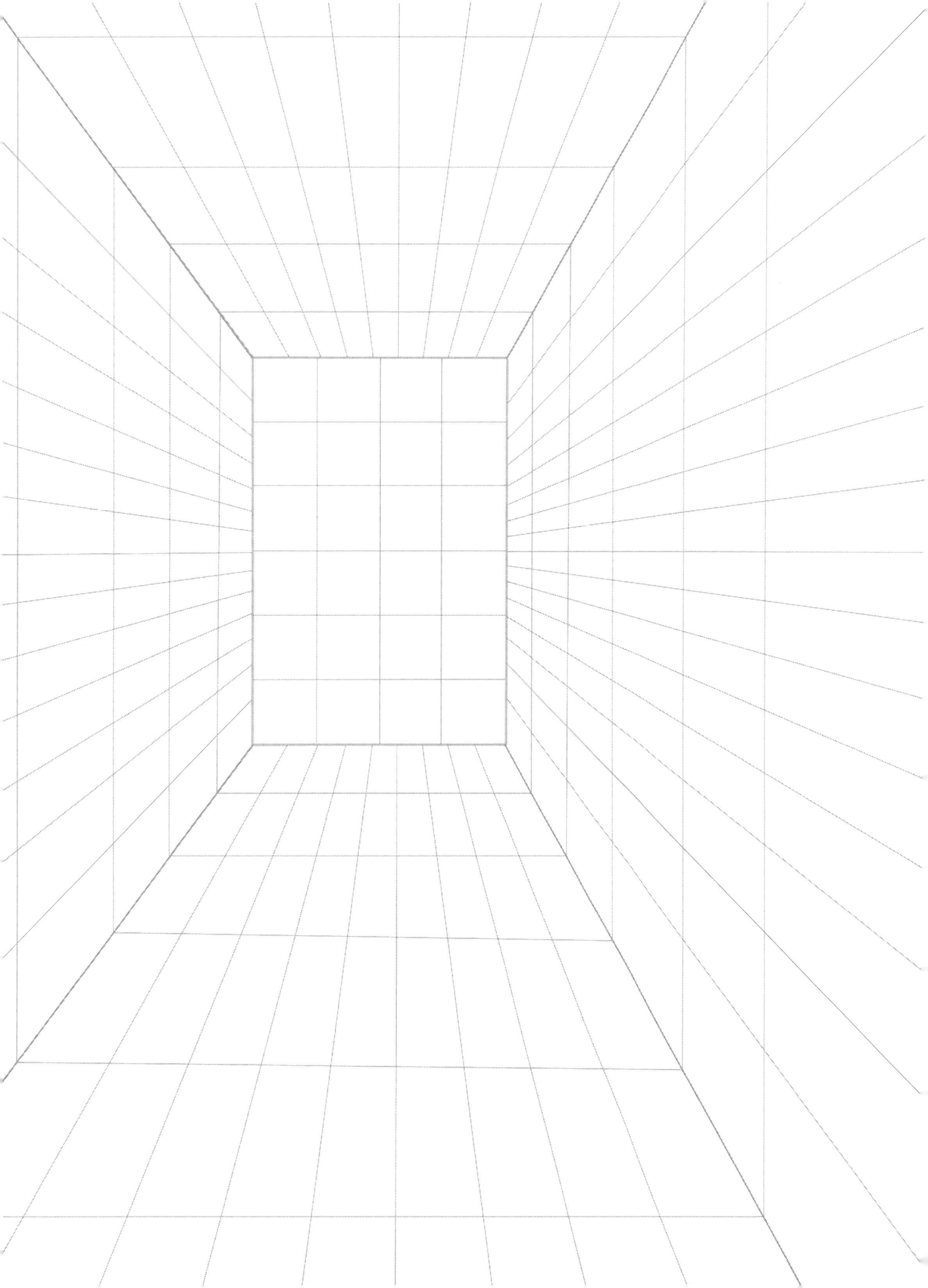

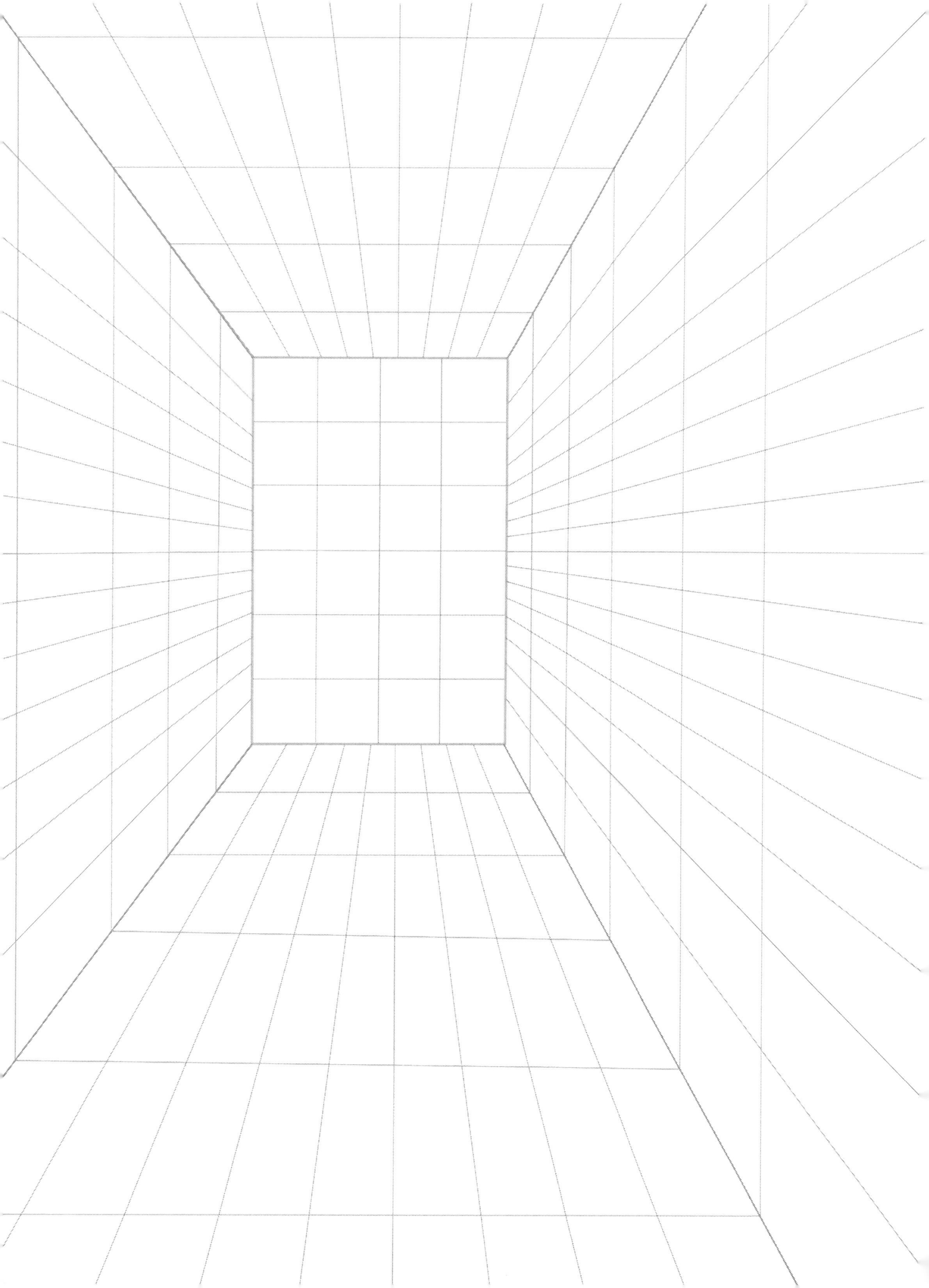

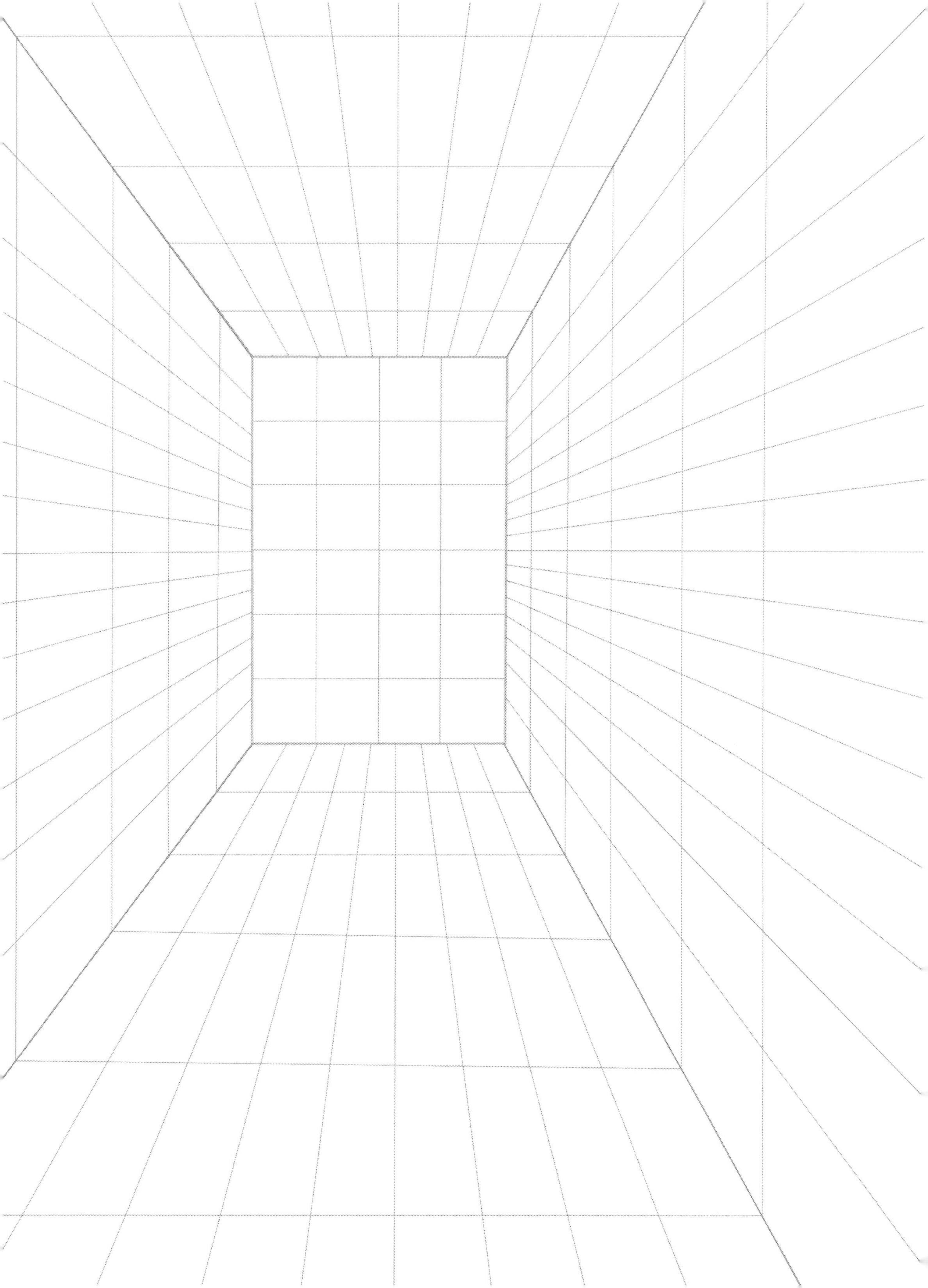

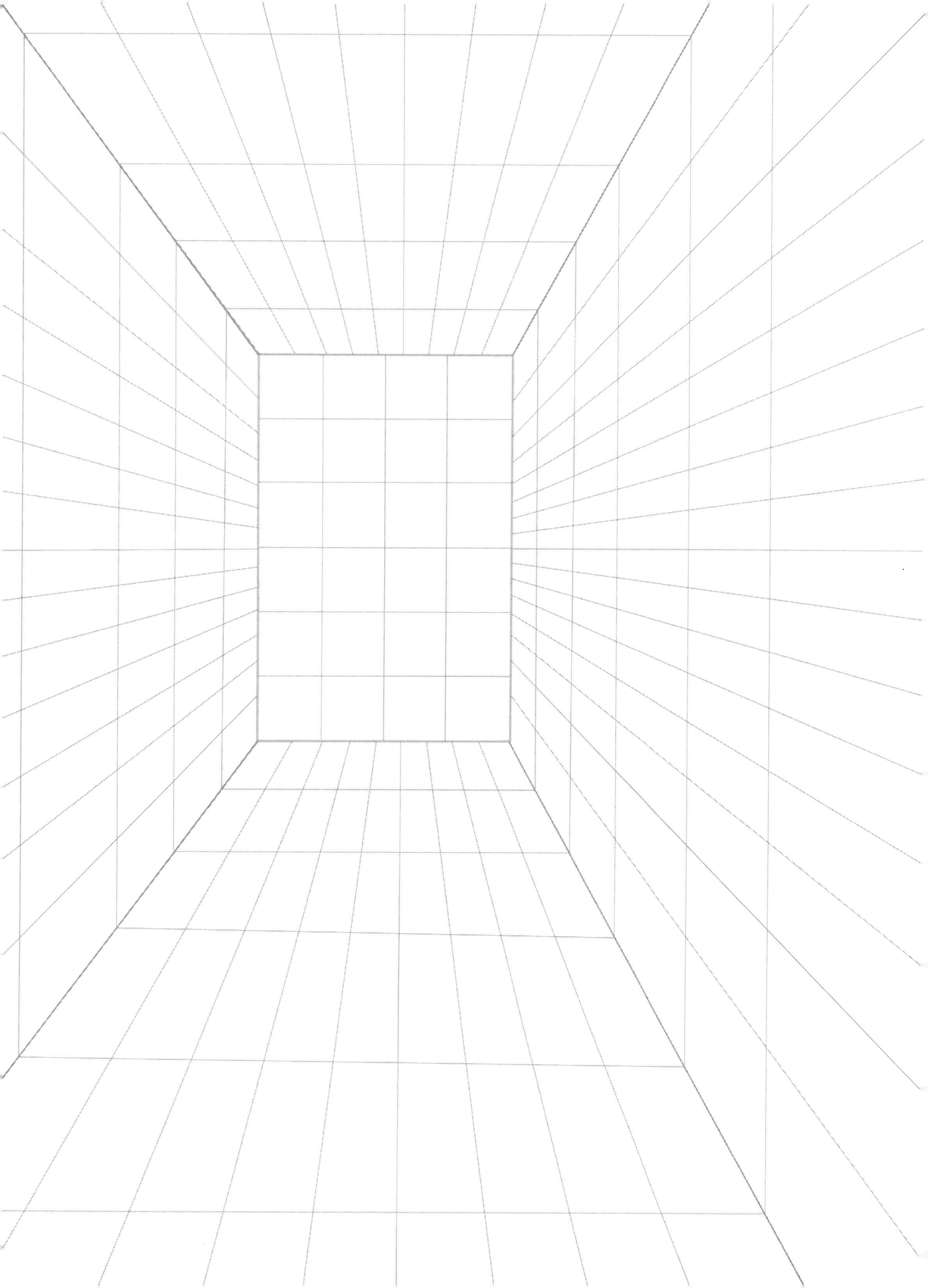

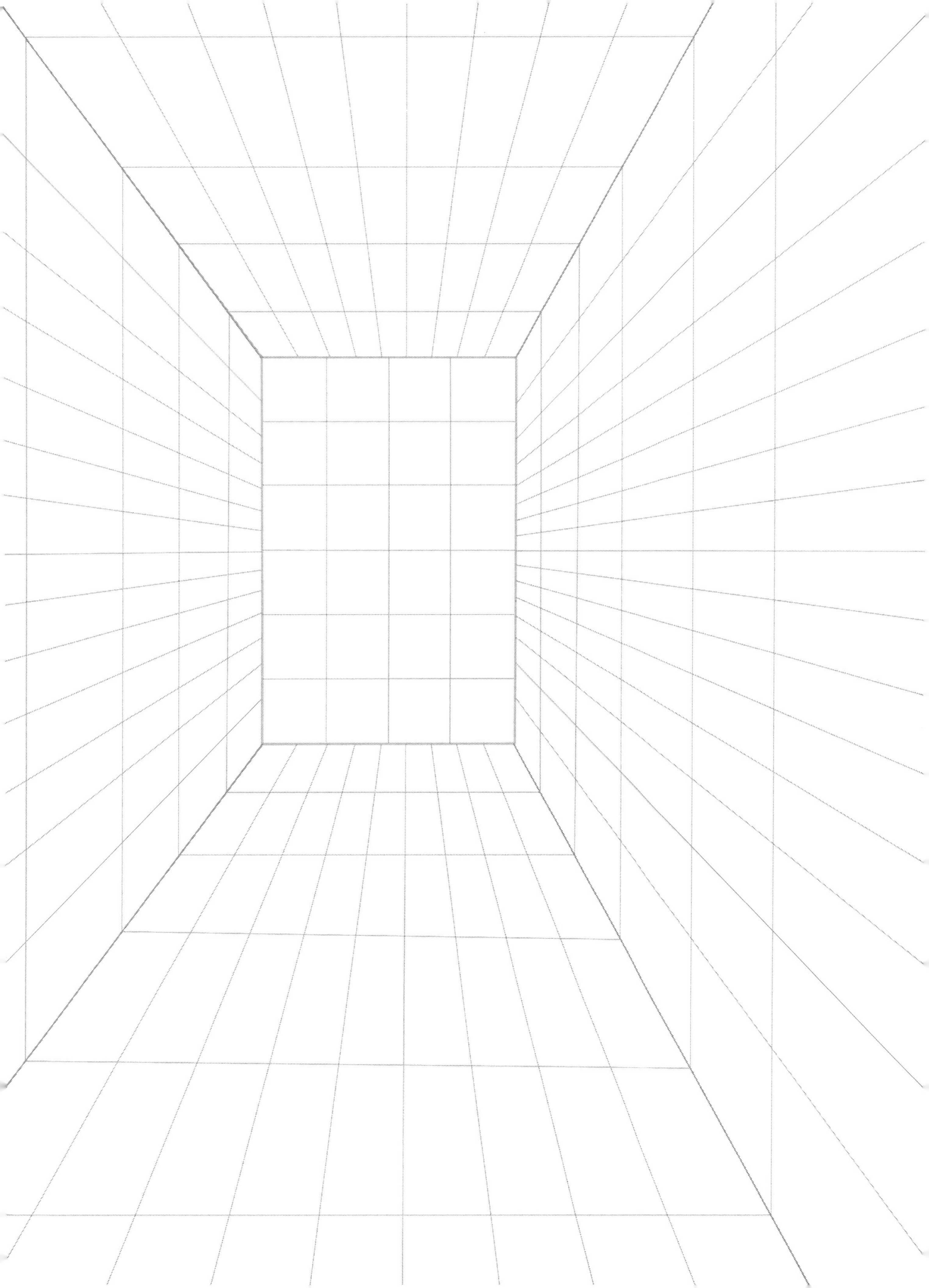

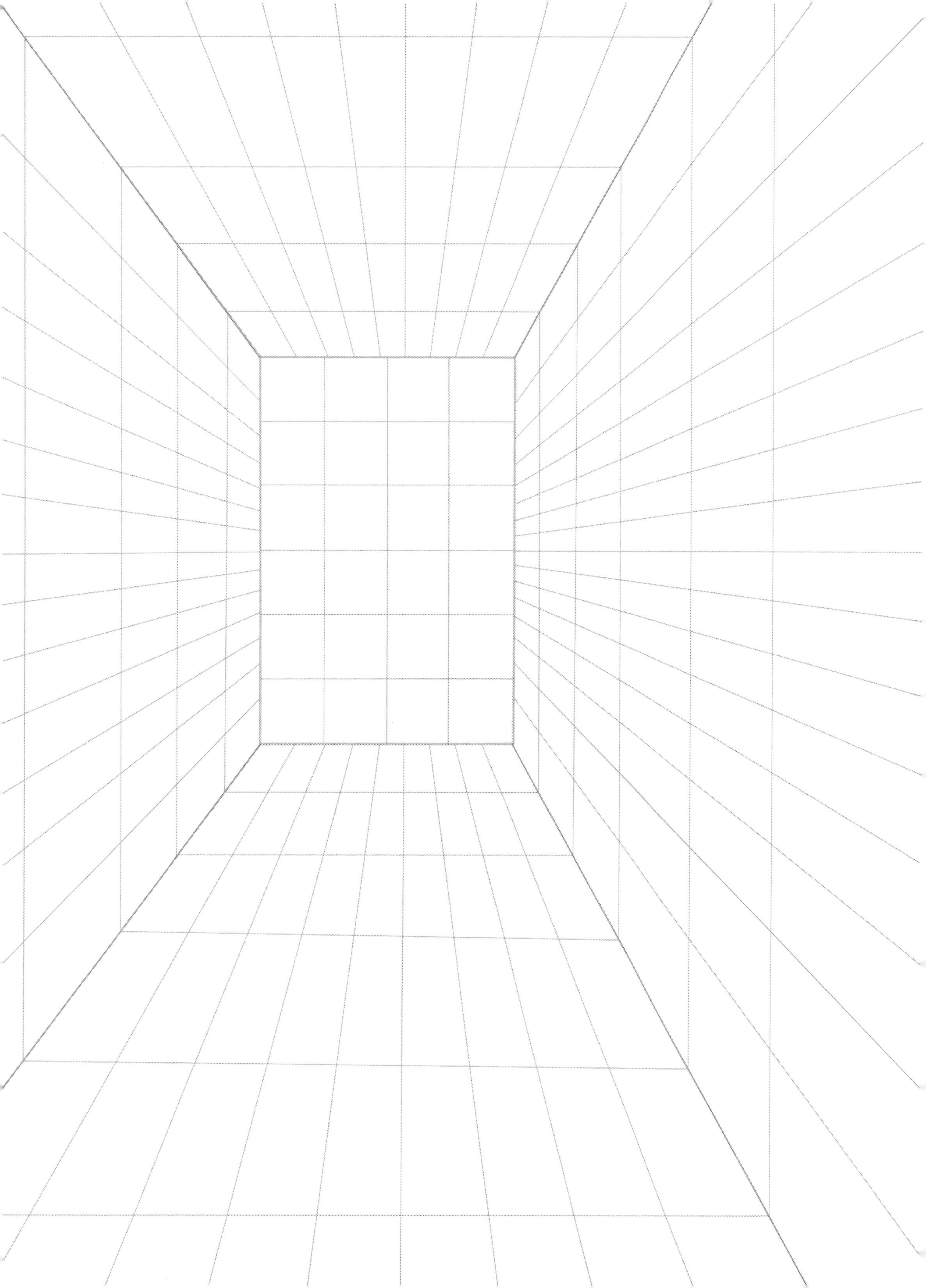

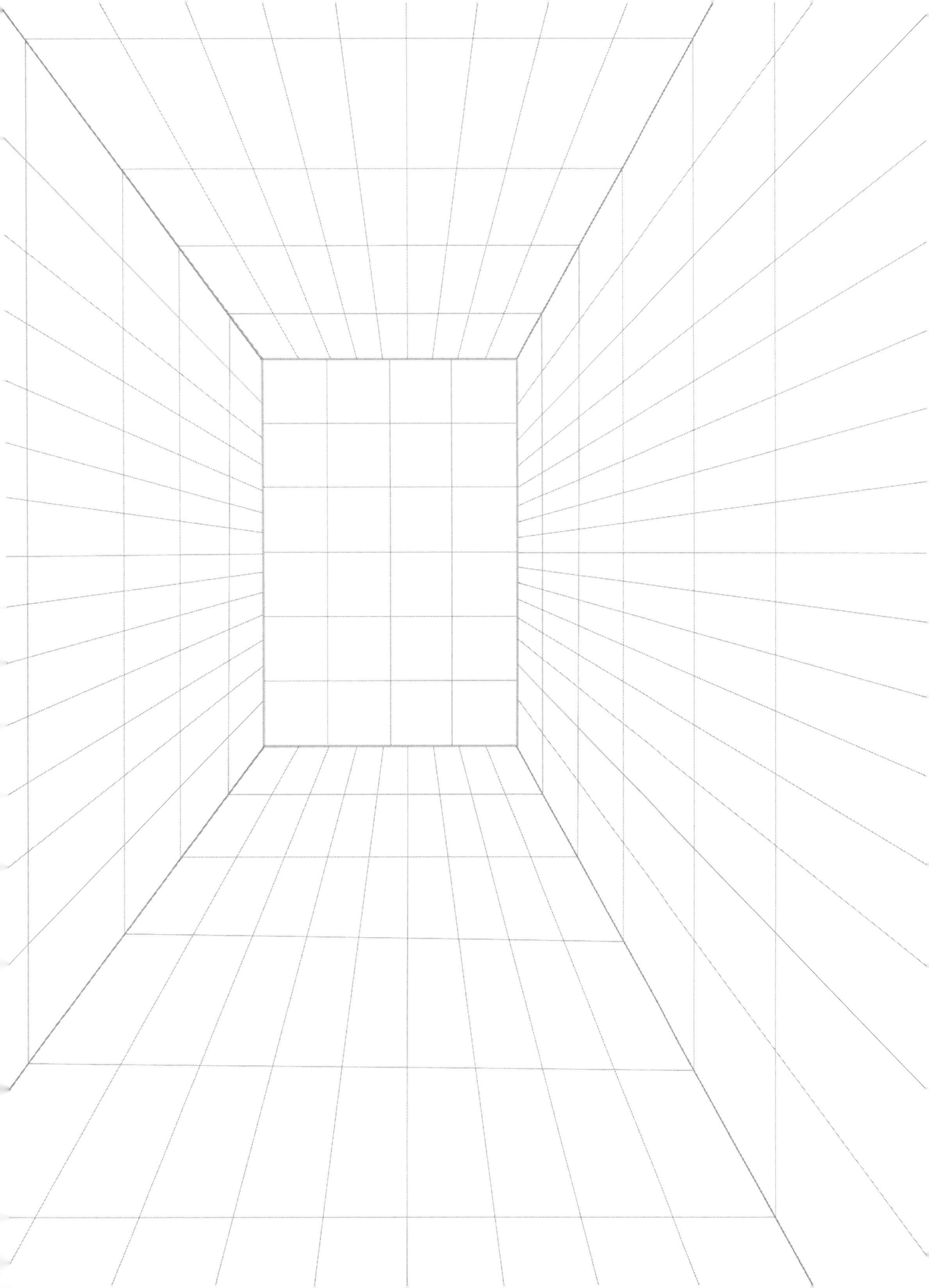

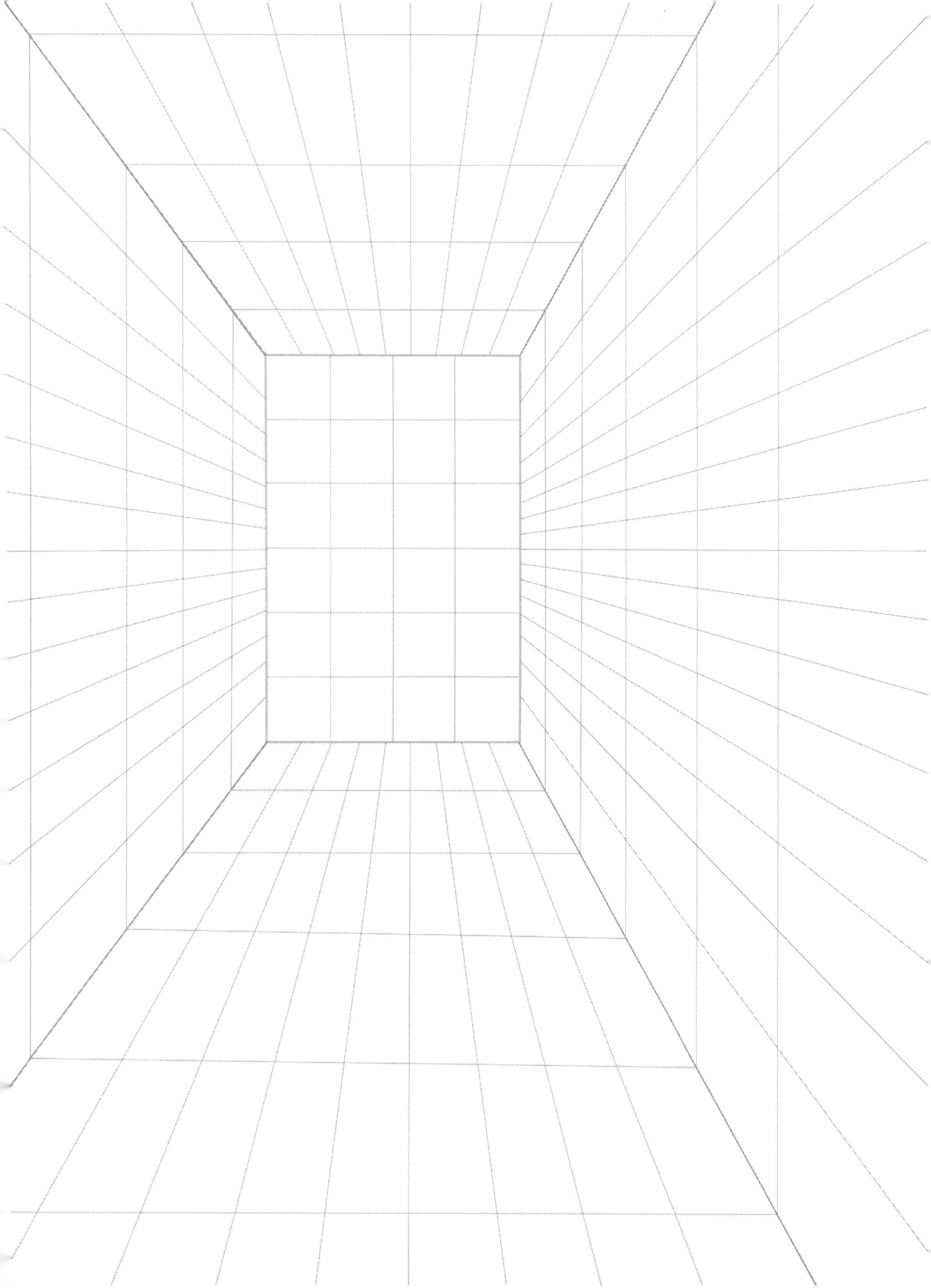

Made in United States
Troutdale, OR
12/05/2023

15378787R00067